Turn left at Goondiwindi

(gun-di-windy)

The book is dedicated to the memory of Susan Elton and Mick Mcdonagh

Contents

Chapter 1 – Turn left at Goondiwindi

Chapter 2 – Wombat

Chapter 3 – Impetus

Chapter 4 – Rookie mistake

Chapter 5 – Dead stuff

Chapter 6 – The city of Dubbo

Chapter 7 – Dubbo to Broken Hill

Chapter 8 – Broken Hill to Ceduna

Chapter 9 – The Eyre Highway

Chapter 10 – On the road, with Whales

Chapter 11 – Skylab

Chapter 12 – Epiphany

Chapter 13 – Heading east

Chapter 14 – The Nullarbor Nymph

Chapter 15 – Nullarbor

Chapter 16 – Port Augusta to Broken Hill

Chapter 17 – One of the food capitals of the world , Gilgandra

Chapter 18 – Last push home

Chapter 19 – conclusions

About the author

References

Chapter 1 – Turn left at Goondiwindi

There is a line in an old song by Rickie Lee Jones that states;

"You never know when your making a memory."

Its so strange what you remember, the memories that hold. My earliest ever memory is when I was four and a half years old, in England in 1963, and my father set off a couple of boxes of fire works in the garage, because it was raining on 'Guy Fawkes' night, and he didn't want to get wet. Alcohol may or may not have been a factor in his decision making. Further on down the line, another memory I have from earlier in my life, is that of watching a travel programme on English TV. It would have had to have been before 2006, as that was the year my immediate family, my wife Raechel, along with daughters Sophie and Grace, and I, up stumps from Essex, UK, and moved to

Brisbane, Australia. The segment of the show I remember involved a chap by the name of Simon Calder, and the memory has always stuck with me.

Now, in those days, back in England, every travel programme seemed to feature Joanna Lumley, usually wearing white cotton slacks, a kimono, and clutching a large glass of chilled Liebfraumilch, smiling broadly into the camera with that "I know it's only 3 pm and I'm already on the hooch, aren't I a pickle" look in her eye. Every week ,when you tuned in, it seemed the show was coming from Salzburg Austria, I'm sure it wasn't, it just seemed that way.

Now, Simon Calder is still around and still working in the travel industry, so I say with respect, that at the time he didn't really fit the profile of what you expected a travel presenter on the BBC to look like. He looked a little geeky, to be honest, like the sort of bloke you would find in a garden shed making computers out of old washing machine parts, and at the weekend, he would probably dress up as a mildly powerful Pokémon.

What I remember of the segment is this;

He flew to Perth, Western Australia, went to a market area where travellers and hippies met to buy and sell items for camping/travelling, purchased a second hand Holden station wagon, and drove to Sydney. Drove across a continent.

No mucking about, no purchase of a desalination unit, no packing his rear axel with extra grease, no Mongolian 'yurt' to sleep in, just a tank of gas and boom, off he went. Drove to Sydney, sold the car and flew back to England.

Wow, I remember thinking, you can do that? Just drive across a country with no preparation? This had always stuck with me, the fact that he just went, drove across Australia. It seemed so audacious.

I'm going to do that one day, I thought, just get in my car and drive, obviously not really believing it. I'm not sure if the memory is completely accurate, but it was along those lines.

(I met Joanna Lumley once, what an utterly charming person.)

Chapter 2- Wombat

When we first arrived in Australia in 2006, and after about a month of car hire, it was down to me to purchase a car. I'm not a car guy, never have been and never will, and apart from the absolute basics, freely admit I know nothing of what goes on under the hood. Not knowing if we were going to make the move to Australia permanent, I didn't really want to purchase a brand new car, I would have to enter the shady world of second hand, but I came up with a cunning plan.

Every now and again the Brisbane City Council would auction off government used cars. At least, I thought ,they would be regularly serviced. So one morning, I took a train to the centre of the city and then got a cab up to the suburb of Zillmere, where the auction was to be held.

I got talking to the taxi driver, explaining to him what I was doing, and then started asking questions about the cab. It was a black Toyota Camry, with over half a million kilometres on the clock. I was astonished, 550,000 kilometres, still going strong, and still being used everyday, wow.

I bought a Toyota Camry at the auction, and drove it home, to an approving nod from my lovely wife. The car was a light green/silver colour and my daughters christened it "Wombat".

The car has stayed with us, and now is nearly 20 years old with 340,000 kilometres on its dial. A few years back my wife treated herself to a VW Golf, so wombat was relegated to the drive way, where years under the Australian sun has played havoc with the paint work, but the car has never given us any problems, never broken down. Maybe she had a good run left inside her, an adventure if you will.

Another reason the car has stayed is my mother in law hates it, so until Wombat physically falls apart into a heap of dust, it's staying.

Chapter 3 - impetus

In 2020 I had a heart attack and had two stents inserted into my heart. According to the surgeon, Dr Gerrard Connors, who saved my life at Greenslopes Private Hospital Brisbane that day, I was knocking on heavens door pretty loudly.

IN 2022 I had a full left knee replacement. When you talk to people about knee replacements, many of them have a little story " My aunty had that done, and she was up cleaning the guttering in 17mins" or, " My husband had that done, and in the evening he performed a tricky Fandango on dancing with the stars". Can I just say to all those people, Fuck Off,... it stings.

So at the age of 64, with body parts wearing out, or in need of replacement, my wife thinking that I was turning into a grumpy wanker, and having recently had two lifelong friends, forever friends, taken by the big C, just weeks after their diagnosis, it was time for me to get off my ever expanding backside, and do something. How about a drive across a continent? It had always been on the back burner, and I now had time to do it. Across the Nullarbor plain that joins Western Australia to South Australia. "You're nuts" said my wife. "In that thing?" gesticulating at wombat. She walked off shaking her head. "But the car had never broken down", I thought, "why would it start now"?

I kept looking at an Australian road map and checking mileage on Google. If I did about 800 km a day, I could go from Brisbane to Dubbo, Dubbo to Broken Hill, and then Broken Hill to Ceduna. Queensland, through New South Wales to South Australia. Then once at Ceduna, which is the start of the Eyre Highway that heads to Perth, WA ,I would head off into the never never and wing it.

I did ask my wife not to say anything to anybody, but well, you know how that goes. I wanted just to get in the car and drive, and deal with problems as they happened, but advice started to be offered.

My friend Matthew Kirk: "Don't stop in Moree, they will have your car up on bricks, and have your tyres off as quick as that", Mrs Jo Johnson: " Have you bought a satellite phone?" Mrs Renae Kirk:" Have you bought an extra spare wheel, so you have two spare wheels?" I love them dearly, but I just wanted to drive. However I did take what I thought were some sensible precautions. I had Wombat serviced at Dave Muller mechanical at Tingalpa Brisbane, [a trustworthy motor mechanic, yes chums, they do exist], joined the RAC, had all the tyres checked, and bought extra engine oil and coolant.

So early one Monday morning, in the middle of September, with the parting comment from my wife "You're being so self indulgent', I loaded the car with a tray of bottled water, and a Tupperware container full of a 2 minute noodle frittata I had made, [which tasted like spongey dry wall], I pulled into the madness that is Brisbane traffic at rush hour. Headed west on the Warrego Highway, around the excellent new bypass at Toowoomba, and with a knot of excitement in my stomach, started to head for Dubbo.

Chapter 4 – Rookie mistake

After 350km west, along the A39, I left Queensland behind and entered New South Wales, I pulled into a rest area for a toilet break. The facilities of which were long drops. To those of you that don't know what long drops are, you are going to have to work that out for yourself, I don't have the stomach to explain.

As I opened the car door, the flies that greeted me were very enthusiastic. These were obviously young apprentice type flies, serving their time outside, near the bins, before being allowed into the inner sanctum of the cubicle.

As you entered, the aroma smacked you in the face like a dead fish. This experience is best summed up by the Australian actor Shane Jacobson in the film Kenny "there is a smell in there that could out last religion", you can't better that line. The flies in the cubicle were different, a totally different attitude, these were old hands. They had done their time outside, and now could relax, sit back a bit, take their feet off the gas. There were flies in there that had gorged themselves so much on human excrement, they had lost the ability to fly.

If the Disney corporation was asked to have a stab at creating an entrance to hell, I'm sure they would send their imagination team over to Australia, and they could lift a few lids on various Long drops, and get some good ideas.

So if it's on your bucket list, and I don't see why it's not on everybody's, to see the walking shit flies of NSW, may I put forward the long drops on the A39 near Boggabilla, it's a good place to start looking.

As I got back in the car, I realised I had left the windows open, big mistake! The car was full of flies, the young energetic ones, They were going on a trip, maybe see some cousins, what an adventure they were about to undertake. As I drove off, to be fair, they did calm down and seemed to rest on the back seat. They only become airborne again five hours later, as I pulled into the carpark of the first hotel of my trip. I wished them well in their new town.

Chapter 5 – Dead stuff

For the majority of my life, I lived in the UK, and have driven all over. I lived for a year in the USA and have driven from the Florida keys to up into Canada, I have driven extensively through France and New Zealand, even had a good drive in South Africa.

Nowhere in the world is there more dead animals by the side of the road than Australia, it is quite unbelievable. Driving down to Dubbo was some of the worse I've seen.

Dead kangaroos ever couple of kilometres, some dead from the night before, and some just lumps of foul smelling ooze that had been baking in the sweltering sun for weeks.

Some looked like they had sat on a pressurised tyre hose and toppled over , arms stretched out as if seeking an embrace. Others looked serene, like they were having a nap, and obviously their were those that had unfortunately been splattered over the road in bits. The smell of dead roo is very piercing, a smell that penetrates every part of your nasal cavities and throat, but on this stretch of road there was some much more carnage.

Dead :

Echidnas

Foxes

Snakes

Wild pigs

Wild boar

Sheep

And, last but not least, an emu with one leg sticking out of it's carcass and into the air at an angle that would be the envy of some dancers at the Moulin Rouge. I'm not sure how much a fully grown kangaroo or boar weighs, but to hit an emu at 110km per hour must be terrifying. Obviously nothing can be done, you can't fence all the roads. It's just shocking, that's all.

Chapter 6 – The city of Dubbo

The city of Dubbo was founded by Sir Francis Dubbo, a novelty plastics manufacturer from the Philippines... that's all nonsense.

The area that modern day Dubbo sits on was first noticed by explorer John Oxley in 1818,who noted that the river and soil would be a favourable place for a settlement. By 1846 there were a number of settlers in the area, so the local government decided to establish a court house, a police station, and a jail.

The town swelled in 1860 when there was a gold rush in Victoria, the state underneath NSW, which brought more travellers coming down from the north. By 1872 the population was 850. It has been suggested that that area had been occupied by Aboriginal people for over 40,000 years. Truly astounding.

No one is sure of the origin of the name Dubbo. It could be an Aboriginal word for "resting place of birds," or 'thubbo' meaning head covering. Or it could be the name of an old Aboriginal man that lived their, no one is sure. Dubbo became a city in 1966, and today 40,000 people live there.

I pulled into the car park of the ibis Budget motel, not expecting much from my experience of a nights rest under its roof, and it didn't let me down. In the lobby, I was third in line, as the computer was having a 'slow' day. By the time the motel employee had processed an air conditioning salesman from Byron bay, there were seven people waiting. The receptionist decided to address us all to save going over hotel protocol numerous times. "That blue door over there" he said pointing, " is locked .It is always locked, you will not get in there late at night, THIS IS FOR YOUR SAFETY'. With that bomb shell, he made eye contact with everyone, as if to make sure we understood the point. He continued." After 8:30pm, the front door of the hotel is locked. Use your room key to gain entry, this is done for your own protection". "Jesus!" I thought, "where were we checking into, Mogadishu?"

After a few more do's and don'ts we were allowed to disperse. In the room, one of the two towels left out for me obviously wasn't fresh. It had that four day old worn underpants feel. Still, my mantra for the trip was 'clean sheets and hot water.' As long as I had those, I would be okay. Anyway, being English, you never complain.

I fancied a stroll, so after getting directions to a supermarket in the centre of town I set off in the gathering dusk. "Doors locked for your safety at 8:30 pm" the chap behind the front counter said with a weary smile as I left. I crossed a long elevated bridge, over a river and what looked like a permanent caravan park. Seemed a bit strange to have one in the centre of town. When I got to the other side I noticed there were a few people setting up what looked like a soup kitchen for the homeless in the carpark of a tyre repair shop. God bless them.

Having found the supermarket I noted that I was probably the only person in there not wearing high visibility work wear. Not a criticism, just an observation. And mullet hair styles seemed to be very popular. Some were marvellously extravagant, as if these hair styles were in training for a large country show. Having got my supplies, I walked out of the shopping centre to find a man shouting at a waste bin. Must have had a good toot on something.

By the time I walked back past the soup kitchen, it was in full swing. It gave the area an edgy feel, and on the walk back across the now pitch black bridge, I looked behind me a few times, to check I wasn't going to get rumbled. Hmm, Dubbo... not to sure about it.

Up early the next morning I made a coffee in my room. Why is it, dear reader, that when making a coffee in any hotel room, with trusted brands on the sachets, it always taste like you are licking Asbestos? One of life's mysteries. As I readied Wombat for departure, I noted that the car next to me, which appeared to be the same one I'd parked next to the previous evening, had had it's windscreen smashed. Not shattered, smashed, as if a hippo had sat on it. Maybe he hit an emu? Not sure if I am thinking of Dubbo as a retirement venue anytime soon. But on this beautiful, sunny day, I was heading north west to Broken Hill.

Chapter 7- Dubbo to Broken Hill

Leaving Dubbo behind I was soon in open country side, wombat purring along. Along the roadside I noticed, obviously apart from the dead roos, there were live goats. Just a smattering to start with, but growing in numbers the further you went away from the town. Some were just scruffy little runt goats, but some were magnificent beasts with elongated curled horns. So magnificent their images could be used on short bread biscuit tins at Christmas time. I didn't see any of them dead; are they more intelligent than kangaroos? Very strange.

Half way to my destination, I stopped in the middle of nowhere, at a place called

Wilcannia for some fuel. Today the town has a population of around 750. Back in the day it was a thriving port on the Darling river, used by paddle steamers transporting mainly wool. In the 1890s, the town had 3000 people living there and 13 pubs. Stretching my legs at the petrol station, all I saw were young Aboriginal people all shouting at each other. Not in an aggressive way, just being really loud. Paying for my fuel I noticed that the servo seemed to be run by a couple of Indian men in their mid-twenties." Why do you live out here?" I asked "money's good," replied Sanjay (that was his name)."Why anybody else would, I don't know. There is a pub, a shop and a garage, and that's it. Its a bit of a mystery." Sanjay continued. "Certainly is." I thought to myself.

On to Broken Hill. What do I know of Broken Hill? I know it's a mining town and a few feature films have been made in the area, Pricilla queen of the dessert and Mad Max 2, being two of them. I cant think of two more conflicting genres of film. Driving into Broken

Hill, it felt as if I was driving into a Western town in the US. Overshadowing the town, and lurking by the side, was the "Line of Load", which is basically a giant slag heap. They have smartened it up at bit, and have put a visitor centre on the top, but it's still a heap of slag from mining. On the top of this you can find the "Line of Load" Miners Memorial. Quite an emotional thing really, dedicated to the 800 souls who have lost their lives to mining in Broken Hill since it began in 1885. The giant Australian mining conglomerate BHP was started here.

In 1883 a sheep station worker named George Rasp, discovered what he thought was tin oxide. In fact it was led, zinc and silver. The ore body he discovered became the largest single source of these materials ever discovered on earth. It has generated over 100 Billion Dollars. Good job old Raspy stubbed his toe on that rock.

I found my motel for the evening without too much trouble. The Argent. It was laid out like a large capital L, with the office at the top of the long side,[a check of which showed it was not manned.] Outside the office there was a metal box on the wall about then size of a microwave oven, where you punched in your mobile phone number and it spat out your room key. AI working there. My room was spotless.

After a shower I thought I'd better check the fluids in Wombat. The car has always had a healthy thirst for oil, which I duly topped up, along with the coolant. Then I noticed a plastic reservoir about the size of a jam jar, which I hadn't seen before, hiding in the corner. After a good wipe with a Wet One," it read "power steering fluid," and it was empty. Was it important? I don't know.

 I looked across the carpark to the motel, and there were a couple of grey nomads sitting outside their motel room, enjoying a cold one. A grey nomad is generally a retired person who spends their time travelling around Australia, typically in a campervan or caravan. "Excuse me, gentlemen, you look like the sort of chaps who know all there is to know about car engines, I wondered if you could take a look at something for me?" It was as if they had been waiting all their lives to hear this request. Their cans of Toohey's New were slammed down, feet were inserted into crocs, and over they came. "is that important?" I asked, pointing to the empty power steering fluid receptacle. It became clear almost immediately that they didn't have a 'Scooby doo' about car engines, but we all agreed that it probably was important, and I should get some.

It was now 4:55 pm, and I didn't have much time to get around town. I didn't want to hang around in the morning until the shops opened at 9am. As the nomads were returning to their table one of them asked, "Where are you heading?" I immediately got embarrassed. Apart from my wife, I hadn't told anyone where I was going. And of course it did seem a bit mad to go across the Nullarbor in an old Toyota. "Adelaide" I lied.

They nodded, satisfied with the answer, and went back to their beer. So started a mad dash around town. The Toyota parts department, which according to the times printed on the door should have been open until 5:30pm, was all shut up at 5:10 pm. I found a car place on the main street "Formula 1" and I could still see people in there. I went in. "Good afternoon, do you have any powering steering fluid for a 20-year-old Toyota?" I enquired. The chap looked at me as if I had asked him to explain Einstein's theory of relativity, but he did get up from his computer and disappeared into a stock room with a passing shout of, "We normally close at 5 pm you know". He reappeared a few minutes later, just as the "Bloke Who Knows Everything", returned to the counter. Every car shop has a BWKE, and my guy asked him if the bottle of liquid he was holding would suit Wombat. "No worries!" he replied. Phew! That's a relief. Then started about 10 minutes of computer keyboard tapping to try and find the price.

"Sorry about this" said BWKE "We break down 5L containers into 1L containers, its a lot easier". Eventually they came up with a price of $15.40. I was already holding $15 in my hand and BWKE said, "That's okay, we will just call it $15". I replied "Thank you, that's very kind, we will call it $15, but I will tip a little bit out". Now for me that was just a silly little throw away line, but for BWKE and his sidekick, it seemed to be one of the funniest things they had heard in a long time. It wouldn't surprise me to hear my comments being recounted Christmas day afternoon after a few sherries. Back at the motel, with Wombat now full of all things liquid, my thoughts turned to my evening meal.

Down the main drag I strolled, my evening shift of flies enjoying the cool air. I popped into Mario's Palace hotel, which had been featured in the Pricilla movie. Neil, the hippy from The Young Ones, was serving, and eventually produced a non alcoholic beer for me. I retired to a corner of the bar. My flies were annoying me. I thought they would wait at the door, but they had joined me inside.

So I finished my drink and carried on down the high street, past some interestingly named streets, Sulphide, Cobalt, Bromide, nice cheery names, and found an Italian restaurant. It was dark by now, so it was okay to eat my pizza in the outside eating area. It was past the flies bed time. All of the shops were shut up and the town felt deserted. I watched the face of the town hall clock, as it kept changing colour every few seconds. It was all very peaceful. "I think I like Broken Hill," I thought.

Chapter 8 – Broken Hill to Ceduna

The next morning I left early, eager to get back on the road. I realised I was suffering from a severe case of get-there-itis. I was heading to Ceduna, the start of the Eyre Highway. It was another beautiful morning, and as I left Broken Hill I noticed a cemetery on the right-hand side. It was truly enormous. "I will investigate that on my way back", I thought.

The vistas on this part of the drive were astoundingly gorgeous. You had 180-degree views and couldn't see any human interference with the landscape. After 50 kilometres, I was stopped at the South Australian border quarantine station, where

I had a pink lady apple confiscated by an officer. You're not allowed to take fruit or veg across the state line for fear of bringing agricultural pests into the state. Further on, I stopped in the town of Peterborough for a coffee stop and toilet break. The previous afternoon in Broken Hill it had been 33 degrees; here in Peterborough, just 280 kilometres away, it was 14 degrees. It was a bit of a shock to the system.

Back into the open country, a constant companion along the drive were wedge-tailed eagles. They use the highway like a large conveyer belt sushi restaurant, serving up fresh roo every morning from the nocturnal accidents that the trucks and cars have with the marsupials. More on the eagles later.

From Peterborough I headed north to Orroroo, then to Wilmington, and on to Winninowie where I picked up the A1 highway, part of the national Highway 1 which connects most of Australia. It is the longest national highway in the world, at a length of 14,500 kilometres. The 'Big Lap', as it's called, can take months to drive, but in 2017 it was completed by a group of guys called Highway One to Hell in record time: five days and 13 hours, in a brand-new Toyota Land Cruiser.

In the last part of this section of the drive you go through the Flinders Ranges – lovely driving, beautiful green hills, and gorgeous views. When you get through the hills, you find yourself in the Port Augusta Renewable Energy Park. There are 50 wind turbines and 250,000 solar panels. Not too sure about putting all these turbines in an area of such natural beauty, but hey, if it slows down the melting of the polar ice caps, I'm in! I followed the A1 and skirted the underside of Port Augusta. At one point, the road splits left to Perth and right to Darwin. It's good to be paying attention at this point. Another five hours on the A1 and I rolled into Ceduna, my home for the night.

After a bit of a faff, I found my hotel and went to check in. The doors to the reception had obviously been repurposed from a 1930s art deco theatre, and as I opened them I saw what looked like an old aquarium full of soda cans. Very strange.

"Hello," said a voice from behind a really tall counter. As I approached, the scene behind the counter unfolded. To my left sat a man I nicknamed Barry – I don't know why, he just looked like a Barry to me – folding terry cloth nappies. In the middle, standing facing me, was the lady who had offered the greeting. Her hair had been scraped back into a severe bun, but some locks had escaped their confinement so it looked like she had licked her finger and stuck it in a plug socket. On the floor to my right was a playpen containing twin 14-month-old boys, not moving and silently watching me. It felt like the start of a Stephen King novel.

I'm sure the children were charming, but they gave me the impression they were thinking, "We're going to remember you, and the next time we meet, we will be carrying knives". All of this went through my mind in an instant before the smell hit. The smell of soiled terry cloth nappies being laundered, it's a smell you don't encounter much anymore, with disposable ones being so readily available. I could feel my nasal hairs melting. It smelt like a hospital in winter, your Nan's slippers, and a vet's flannel, all rolled into one.

"Will you be joining us for complimentary continental breakfast in the mornings?" asked Mrs Plug Socket. Still trying to hold my breath, I shook my head, grabbed my keys and exited the theatre doors.

The hotel had all the charm of a correctional facility. I knew I would encounter various standards of motel on this trip, but I found this one just depressing. On the plus side it was in the right position, at the start of the Eyre highway. It had hot water, clean sheets and coffee sachets that tasted like tile grouting; I would survive.

What surprised me were the other guests' cars parked outside their rooms. There were Lexuses, top-of-the-range Land Cruisers, and four-wheel drive jobs that had been fitted with all sorts of camping attachments. All very expensive vehicles. Wombat looked a little self-conscious, to be honest.

After a shower, I drove into town for a stickybeak (UK equivalent, a butcher's; USA translation, a look). The town gave me the impression it was slowly dying: empty shops, groups of youngsters hanging around with nowhere to go. I stopped at the Visitor Information Centre and had the good fortune to speak to Sandy. Lovely lady; I do hope these people get paid and are not just volunteers. She could not have been more helpful. I asked various questions about my drive for the next day and she warned me about buying petrol at the Nullarbor Roadhouse, where it's over $3 per litre. Ay caramba! Fair enough, you're going to be in the middle of nowhere, but that is a bit steep. But hey, what are you going to do? Not even Bear Grylls can make petrol. Although on second thought, he probably can. So, taking Sandy's advice, I would aim for a truck stop at a place called Cocklebiddy after first stopping at a whale watching opportunity at the head of the Great Australian Bight. Ceduna to Cocklebiddy is about 800 kilometres, and my stop for whale watching was about 300 kilometres from the start. Excellent.

The next morning I awoke at 5 am, so eager to get back on the road that by 5:30 am I was back on the highway. It was still pitch dark, and it started to rain. At the age of 64, I've noticed that things get a little fuzzy when driving at night, my eyes not focusing like they used to. Things were certainly intense when I was passing oncoming road trains. I'm pretty sure road trains only operate in Australia, and are the longest trucks in the world, some 60 metres long. That's the length of 12 average cars. Think of a truck pulling three shipping containers, you'll get the idea. Eventually dawn broke behind me as I headed west. I noticed that the roadkill was a bit different.

Along with the obligatory kangaroos, there were other carcasses – wombats. My lovely wife adores the majority of Australian wildlife, she can do without snakes, and has a particular fondness for wombats. I once took her to the Cradle Mountain area of Tasmania just to see wild wombats. They were very cute; they were the sort of animals you wanted to pick up and snuggle.

The wombats of the Nullarbor are the southern hairy-nosed variety, and seemed much bigger and more muscular than their cute island cousins. These weren't Hugh Grants, these were Russel Crowes (not that I want to snuggle Hugh Grant, but hopefully you're following my analogy). So, off I went, on the Eyre Highway, across the Nullarbor Plain, across the Australian continent.

Chapter 9 – The Eyre Highway

The Eyre Highway is a 1,664-kilometre road linking Western Australia to South Australia, which runs over the Nullarbor Plain. It goes from Port Augusta, in SA, through Ceduna, and then on to Norseman in WA.

Before WWII the route was just a dirt track, rarely used by vehicles. With the impending war looming, the Australian government thought it might be a good idea to connect various parts of Australia to one another. The finished road, whilst a massive improvement on the previous route, was still just a dirt track, subject to flooding and other natural elements. They started to seal the road in 1960, and eventually finished it in 1976. Because some sections are so remote, parts of the highway serve as emergency landing strips for the Royal Flying Doctor Service. I love that. The road was named the Eyre highway in 1943, after Western Australia and South Australia agreed on the name honouring early English explorer

Edward John Eyre. He became the first European to cross the Nullarbor in 1840–1841. To say that Eyre had a diverse life is a little bit of an understatement. Here is his story, some of which, my dear Australian readers, is not brilliant, to be honest. I will let you make your own mind up.

Born in Bedfordshire, England, in 1815, Edward John Eyre left as a 17-year-old and journeyed to Australia to 'prove himself'. He involved himself in cattle and sheep farming, and after driving sheep and cattle overland from Monaro, New South Wales, to Adelaide, South Australia, he used the profits to fund exploration expeditions into the interior of Australia. After finding out that some cattle owners were going to try and take a herd of cattle over to Western Australia, he suggested they pay him to go first and map out a route. He was aiming to get to Albany on the southern coast of Western Australia, the first ever settlement in that enormous state – a journey of some 2,500 kilometres. (If Western Australia was a country, it would be the 10th largest country in the world, knocking Algeria down into 11th.)

In June 1840, he set out with an Aboriginal man named Wylie, whom he had befriended, English friend John Baxter, and two other young Aboriginals, Joey and Yarry. The expedition was beset by many problems, finding water and food being the main concerns. Obviously in the back of Eyre's mind was the hope the Indigenous members of the party would help with those problems. At one stage, to offset starvation, they ate one of their horses. At another, Wylie found a dead penguin on the seashore and promptly ate it. One night, whilst Eyre and Wylie were out foraging for food, the two young Aboriginal boys shot Baxter dead and ran off with the supplies that were left. Very near to death, Eyre and Wylie had the fortune of finding the French whaling ship *Mississippi*, under the captainship of Englishman Thomas Rossiter, moored in an area where the town of Esperance now stands. They stayed on board for two weeks to rest and regain their strength. Rejuvenated, and with fresh supplies, they pressed on with their journey, arriving in Albany on the 7th of July 1841. Eyre returned by ship to Adelaide and received a hero's welcome. He was awarded the Royal Geographical Society's gold medal. In the Adelaide region, he was appointed magistrate and protector of the Aboriginal people, where for three years he quelled any violence or problems in that frontier region.

After that commission, he became Lieutenant Governor of New Zealand in 1846, and in 1864 he was appointed Governor of Jamaica, in the Caribbean. This is where the story gets a little sticky.

As the Governor, apparently Eyre only had contact and concerns with the white ruling classes and the estate owners, whose interests he was sympathetic to. He did nothing to try and relieve unemployment or tax burdens of the native Jamaicans and poorer classes. After his time looking after the Aboriginal people in Australia, to me, this seemed very out of character. George Gordon, a member of the assembly of Jamaica, criticised Eyre's leadership in parliament. "If we are to be governed by such a governor much longer, the people will have to fly into arms and become self-governing". Baptist preacher Paul Bogle stirred things up even more and led to a rebellion that resulted in the killing of 18 officials and militia. Eyre's response was quick and decisive, and he began 'an orgy of reprisals', leaving 608 dead, the flogging of 600 and the burning of 1,000 homes. Included in the people dead were Gordon and Bogle, two of 14 people he had hung for treason.

The European settlers of Jamaica thought him a hero as they still had their land, their property, and their lives. You can probably guess what the local workers thought of him.

Back in England, his actions caused an almighty legal uproar. You either agreed with his actions or didn't, and he was immediately called back to England. There were calls for Eyre to be arrested and tried for murder. The Jamaica Committee was set up to demand his prosecution. Many English liberal intellectuals, including Charles Darwin, joined. On the flip side, the Governor Eyre Defence and Aid Committee was set up to argue the Eyre had acted decisively to restore order. Charles Dickens and poet Alfred Tennyson were members.

He faced court three times and was exonerated of all charges. One of the judges remarked he had acted with "commendable promptitude". Eyre's legal expenses were covered by the English government. He retired on a colonial governor's pension to Devon, UK, where he saw out his days. There are statues of Eyre in Adelaide and New South Wales, and his name lives on in places such as Lake Eyre, Eyre Peninsular, Eyre Creek, John Eyre High School and an electoral district in Western Australia. There has even been an opera about him. In Jamaica, I can find nothing that bears his name.

Whether or not the naming committees of the highways and byways in the 1940s knew of his later life exploits, I'm not so sure. Whether or not I am being swayed by today's political correctness, it just leaves me feeling a little uneasy. Still, on with the adventure.

Chapter 10 – On the road, with whales

Having left Ceduna, and in what seemed to be no time at all, I was directed off the highway to the whale watching centre at the eastern end of the Bunda Cliffs. $18 to stand on a wooden viewing platform? Hmmm. Okay, I guess. Whale watching on the Nullarbor, who would have thought it? I certainly didn't. There was a family behind me, and gramps was certainly not happy with having to cough up $45 for a family pass. Now where I live, in Brisbane, we are so lucky that very close to us is the beautiful North Stradbroke Island where, during the whale-watching season (June until November), around 30,000 humpback whales migrate past the island. My wife and I have spent many hours watching these magnificent animals, so I have a pretty good idea of what to look for. At first glance that morning, I couldn't see a thing. And then, boom, a mother and calf southern right whale, so close that I could have hit them with a tennis ball. The southern right whale is so called because it was made of the right stuff, i.e. oil to burn in lamps. In the early 1800s there were thousands and thousands of them in the southern oceans. Within 200 years, man had nearly killed them all. Luckily, with the banning of commercial whaling, they are increasing in numbers, and they use the shallows bays off South Australia to teach their young calves to swim. I truly love seeing them.

After an hour or so, I jumped back into Wombat and pointed her west. When you look at a map of the area you see all these names along the highway: Madurra, Mundrabilla, Caiguna, etc. I expected them to be small communities, but in reality they are just truck stops. They all have motel rooms, a restaurant, a gift shop and overpriced fuel. In fact, everything is way overpriced. I was stopped at the South Australian/Western Australian border, and was again questioned by highway officers to see if I was carrying fruit or vegetables. Before I entered Western Australia, I pulled into Border Village, which is a truck stop. I refuelled Wombat, checked the air in the tyres, and purchased a coffee that I hoped didn't taste like I was licking the bottom of a budgie's cage. I made the mistake of ordering a pre-made sandwich. I'm not sure when it was made, but I think Japan had just surrendered.

All of the staff in these truck stops were foreign students/traveller types, and Jürgen (German), took three goes to get me the right sandwich. Maybe it was his first day; be nice. I'm sure if I had ordered a bratwurst with a side order of schnitzengruben, it wouldn't have been a problem. As I expected, the cheese sandwich was a major disappointment – so dry I had to keep taking small sips of coffee just to be able to chew it. It was like trying to eat Gandhi's flip-flop. Still, I didn't complain; I'm English. I had the briefest of looks around the gift shop, at the fly swats, the t-shirts, and the optimistically-priced $20 tin of spam, and I was back on the road.

What was I expecting of the road? I thought it was going to be driving through a desert. It's not. I thought I would call into a truck stop to find Peter O'Toole at the bar, in dusty khaki clothes, cradling a gin and tonic, with watery eyes saying, "I've just come in from the never never," but it's not like that at all. The scenery changes constantly, from small shrubs to trees, to burnt trees, and back to shrubs and everywhere in between. And, you see, you're not really driving. With so few trucks and cars on the road, sitting with my knees under the steering wheel and my hands resting lightly above them, and with the cruise control on, you just sort of point the car and go. You had 180 degrees of vision, you could look anywhere, and the car would keep going straight. Well, almost.

You don't have to go too far across the Nullarbor to find civilisation, which surprised me. I think the furthest you can go between truck stops is 190 kilometres – not too far at all, really. I filled up every time my fuel gauge read half. I knew that the top half of my fuel indicator gave me between 500 and 600 kilometres, depending on the headwind. If it went below a half, the petrol would disappear quicker than Chris Chippendale downing a pint of Stella when he realised someone else is going to buy a round. (I know you don't know Chris Chippendale, but believe me when I say this analogy is accurate, and mildly amusing. I promise.)

From Border Village, at the WA border, to Cocklebiddy, my stop for the night, was 284 kilometres (three hours). After 100 kilometres on the road, I passed a truck stop at Mundrabilla. Small story time.

Mundrabilla used to be a sheep station, founded in 1872 by two brothers, Thomas and William Kennedy, and friend William McGill. They had trekked 1,200 kilometres from Albany, WA, with 1,500 head of sheep. At Mundrabilla, they found decent pasture and water, and decided to settle. Back in those days, life was a tough existence. McGill's wife died during childbirth, and Kennedy was speared to death. Today, the Mundrabilla Roadhouse sits about 35 kilometres from the original homestead, with cattle being the main concern.

The point of the tale: a little north of the truck stop, the largest meteorite ever found in Australia was discovered. The first fragments of rock were discovered in 1911 by camel foreman Harry Kent, but in 1966 two large boulders were found by geologists R Wilson, and A Cooney. The largest of the rocks, very imaginatively named Mundrabilla 1 (not sure how they came up with that) weighed in at 12,400 kg. It is the 11th largest meteorite ever found on earth, with the second rock, (yes, you've guessed it) Mundrabilla 2, in at number 16, with a weight of 6,100 kg.

Thought to be 60 million years old, and being the metallic core of an asteroid that broke up on entry into the earth's atmosphere, the meteorites may have been laying on the plains – are you ready for this, ladies and germs? – for one million years.

The outback of Australia is truly a magical and mysterious place. A wee bit hot at times, but you can't have everything.

Just for your interest, the largest meteorite discovered so far on Earth is the Hoba, in Namibia, south-west Africa. Weighing in at nearly 64,000 kg, it was discovered by farmer Jacobus Brits when he hit it with his plough in 1920. The meteorite is now a national monument, and has never been moved because it's too heavy. Would you believe, back in the day, it was vandalised? Someone with a handsaw took about 5 hours to hack a piece off. In 2021, at Bonhams auction house in Los Angeles, the 2.8 kg lump of the Hoba was sold for $59,000 American. Humanity, Jesus.

***

After another couple of hours, I rumbled into the Wedge tail Inn at Cocklebiddy. I had no phone connection and was in a different time zone, 45 minutes behind what I had on my watch. Two young ladies were on duty in reception, one Italian and one French, who I quickly nicknamed Florence and Antoinette.

They went through motel protocol, and then wanted a $10 deposit off me for the TV remote. Seemed strange. Do people pinch TV remotes from motels in the middle of nowhere? I was directed to my room, which was in a far block. I drove around, and as I parked I noticed, bizarrely, there were three gyrocopters parked side by side. It was as if Daniel Craig had popped in with couple pals for a weekend of … not sure, really, maybe some dry sandwich eating. Mind you, he's English, so he wouldn't have complained.

Cocklebiddy was an Aboriginal religious mission back in the day, but is now just a truck stop, actually right where you need one. I checked into my room. The first thing I saw when I opened the door and my eyes adjusted to the gloom was a can of Raid insect killer, about the size of a scuba tank. "Good first impression," I thought. Light yellow paint had been applied to the brick walls. The TV antenna (an old-school TV antenna, the ones that used to sit on top of the TV with metal poles at a 10 to 2 angle) was screwed into the brickwork two feet above the telly. The carpet, if in fact it was carpet, was worn down to nothing, so you were actually walking on green concrete. The pièce de résistance was the gold-coloured metallic scouring pad ceiling tiles. It was so appalling it was brilliant (more on the ceiling tiles later.) Whereas the motel the night before in Ceduna had been depressing, this was fun. I had a shower and, as expected (and fair enough, you're in the middle of nowhere), the pressure of the water resembled an 87-year-old man with prostate problems' urine flow. (Not that I know what that looks like; I just imagined that analogy.)

I got changed and dabbed a little bit of one of Beckham's many fragrances for men behind my ears. I think this one was called 'Sunrise over Billingsgate fish market'. Not that I thought I would meet Emma Watson or Kirsten Stewart in the cocktail bar before dinner, I just thought it may keep the flies away. I came out of my room to find Wombat at a funny angle. Poo, arse, wank and shit. Flat tyre, driver's side, back. Not a tyre needing a bit of air, no sir; a flat. When I weighed up my options, I realised I didn't have any.

So, I got changed back into grubby gear and started rolling around in the dust. David Beckham's scents for men, let me tell you, are no good for fly control. With a fair bit of swearing and a bit of brute force I managed to get the tyre changed, noting that when I had the wheel off there was a definite crunching sound coming from the axle. As I've said before, I am no mechanic, but I have seen *Wheeler Dealers* enough times to know that Wombat could have smashed wheel bearings. I also checked the fluids, and the oil was bone dry. "Impossible," I thought, "I checked it yesterday. Very healthy." I checked it half a dozen times, completely bone dry. Where the hell did all of that go? Anyway, I had taken the precaution of bringing spare engine oil with me (pat on the back, there), so I topped up Wombat, showered again, then wandered into the dining room to peruse the menu du jour. I really wasn't expecting much, and it didn't let me down.

The restaurant was packed. Antoinette was waitress for the evening, and she minced around like she was handbag shopping on the Champs-Élysées. After 10 minutes I caught her eye, and she seemed generally surprised that I wanted to see a menu. All of the usual suspects of roadside dining in Australia were there: roast dinners, burgers, crumbed lamb cutlets, etc. I ordered a chicken schnitzel with chips. As I waited for my order to arrive, Antoinette was taking the order of a grey nomad couple sitting in front of me. "What's the fish of the day?" the female nomad asked. Now, fair enough, in bold type on the menu it had stated, somewhat optimistically, "Catch of the Day". I'm not sure if, before her question, she had considered the logistics of getting fresh fish 700 kilometres from the coast to the obviously highly-trained chefs at the Wedge tail, on a daily basis.

Still, I'm sure the arrival of the fish van [if it exists], goes something like this:

"Bruce, Terry the fish is here."

"Hello, mate. What have you got for us today?"

"Some large baldchin groper, a blue morwong, and a couple of estuary cobblers."

"Lovely, I'll take the lot. I feel a bouillabaisse coming on."

I'm sure that's what happens. I'm sure that if anybody orders fish here, the chef doesn't just open a chest freezer and dip into a cardboard box with "New Zealand Hoki portions" written on the side. Anyway, back to the story.

Antoinette was taking the order. "What's the fish of the day?" asked the lady traveller. Antoinette thought for a moment, gave one of those famous French shrugs, and answered, "I don't know, it's white." This seemed to appease the nomad, and she duly ordered the fish. I'm glad it was white.

My dinner arrived. At first, I thought they had fried a baseball cap of a supporter of Max Verstappen. This sort of dark orange, curled up, deep fried tube was placed in front of me. Even the chips looked embarrassed. It was served with a steak knife. Antoinette dumped and fled. After a bit of sawing, I got a mouth-sized morsel prepared and bit into it. Lovely, warm cooking oil filled my mouth. Still, I'm English; I'm not going to complain.

I went to bed that night a concerned man.

Would the spare tyre still be inflated in the morning?

Would the back axle break?

Did I have a major oil leak?

No phone coverage for 400 kilometres. (I wish I'd bought a satellite one.)

Would I get another puncture? (I wish I had bought two spare tyres.)

Who played the Tin Man *The Wizard of Oz*?

How does the bloke who drives the snowplough get to his work?

What happened to Old Zealand?

All of these questions were whirling around in my head as I lay there, staring at the gold metallic ceiling tiles.

The next morning, I returned the remote. As I discovered there were only two channels to choose from anyway, and one of them made everything look like it was in a snowstorm, I didn't really need the remote at all. If you ever want to watch test cricket in the snow, this is the place. I checked Wombat carefully. Tyre was still inflated, and no oil under the car. So, I pulled gingerly onto the highway for the last 400 kilometre stretch to Norseman, the end of the Eyre Highway.

I was nervous. It wouldn't be a major problem if I broke down, someone would stop and help, but it would be a pain. And, of course, it would give my wife the ammunition to say "I told you so".

I set Wombat's cruise control to 98 km/h, the speed she seemed happiest at, and pointed west. The road was excellent. Open plain in front of me, and soon my worry of mechanical issues eased and I enjoyed the drive. After two hours, I called in to the Balladonia truck stop for a car check and to grab a coffee. As I was waiting my turn for the tyre hose, something caught my eye. On top of the roadhouse was a piece of sheet metal about the size of a large dining table, with some stencilled numbers and holes in it, and the word 'Skylab'. That set a very small bell ringing in the back of my head. Skylab? I had heard of that word before. Wasn't it something the Americans threw up into space? What the hell was that doing on a truck stop in the middle of nowhere on the Nullarbor Plain?

After checking the car, all seemed well. I went in to buy a coffee. As I made my order, just inches away to my right, in one of those heated glass display units, were the most seductive, gorgeous-looking sausage rolls I think I've ever seen. These weren't the six inches of goo in cellophane you see in 7-Eleven, no sir. These were out of the bag. They had style, prominence, gravitas. They were playful, yet dignified; flirty, yet serious. They knew how brilliant they were, but played their brilliance down. These were the

Sandra Bullocks of the sausage roll world. I bought one. It could have been a dozen, but I didn't want to deprive the other travellers. And, as I waited for the South American student to perk my coffee, I noticed there was a small museum at the end of the building. In I went, trailing sausage roll crumbs behind me like confetti, and there, in the corner, was the full story of Skylab.

Chapter 11 – Skylab

Skylab was the United States of America's first orbiting space station, and one of the biggest things they have flung into space. It launched on the 14th of May 1973 (my 14th birthday), and re-entry was 11th July 1979. It was visited by three different astronaut crews, and was occupied for a total of 24 weeks whilst in orbit. On board was a solar and earth observatory and a workshop/lab for hundreds of experiments that they carried out. It was hoped that Skylab would stay in orbit until the space shuttle had been developed, which could then help boost Skylab's orbit. Sadly, delays in the shuttle's development meant that Skylab was on its own, and its orbit began to crumble.

Now, for the bods at NASA, this was a major headache. 77,000 kg of hot metal crash-landing into, say Madrid, New Delhi or, worse still, Milton Keynes, could cause a few negative headlines. They tried to adjust the Skylab's re-entry orbit so that it crashed into the sea off of South Africa, but the spacecraft didn't break up like they thought it would and it did a few more orbits. Eventually it came down over the bottom left-hand corner of Australia, over the township of Balladonia. The very small community, nine people in total, was about to become the centre of a global media scrum. The guests at the motel reported seeing what reminded them of a fireworks display from the Royal Show. Various chunks of metal from the exploding spacecraft laded nearby. At one point, the then President of the United States, Jimmy Carter, phoned the owner of the roadhouse to offer apologies. In the coming days the local council issued NASA with a tongue-in-cheek $400 littering fine. Brilliant. Reporters from around the globe descended on this outback spot in droves. Miss America, at a pageant in Perth at the time, was sent in for a publicity stunt. Media personnel were fighting over the one phone line, to be in time to make deadlines.

The San Francisco Examiner newspaper set a prize of $10,000 for the first person who brought an authentic piece of Skylab to their offices within 72 hours, obviously thinking that it would be unachievable. In those days, in 1979, it was still the heyday of great rivalries between newspapers.

You've seen the old films with the editor in the corner office, with bright braces holding up his trousers, sleeves rolled up, receding hairline slicked back, cigar stub hanging out of the corner of his mouth, shouting "Hold the front page!" Well, in San Francisco, the *Examiner* was right next door to the *Chronicle.* They shared the same print room and were great rivals, each trying to get as many paying readers as possible. There was an unwritten law that you couldn't use what the other paper was going to say, but sometimes it was impossible not to notice what the other paper was going to print. The *Chronicle* was going to offer $200,000 USD to anybody who was injured by the falling spacecraft. The *Examiner* had to come up with something quick; that's how they came to offer $10,000 USD for the first piece of genuine Skylab to arrive at their offices within three days. They took the precaution of phoning NASA to see if they were safe to offer the monetary incentive. "Go ahead, offer the money," was the response.

The day of the re-entry dawned. Some tourists on the British coast sheltered in caves. In Belgium, the government readied air horns to warn residents to take shelter. A Brazilian woman who had given birth on the day had called her child Skylab, in the hopes NASA would help pay for its upbringing. In the Philippines, a man died of a heart attack, shouting "Skylab! Skylab!" as he awoke from a nightmare.

In Times Square, New York, you could buy 'Skylab survivor' T-shirts and hats with targets on them. In St Louis, Missouri, the 'Skylab Watchers and Gourmet Diners Society' planned to watch Skylab's last orbit at a garden party, where "hard hats, or similar protective headgear" was required for entry. In Charlotte, North Carolina, a local hotel had painted a large target on the roof and hosted a disco pool party. One enterprising individual even started selling cans of pressurised 'Skylab repellent'.

Four-wheel drive outback types were descending on the Nullarbor scrub in droves, trying to get in on the action, searching for parts of the spaceship. In the end, Stan Thornton, a 17-year-old from Esperance, [roughly 200km away from Balladonia as the crow flies,] miraculously managed to claim the prize. Small parts of debris had landed on his mum's shed roof, and, with the help of a Perth radio station and Qantas, he flew to the United States.

Such was the need for speed, he didn't even have time to pack a suitcase; all he had with him was a sandwich bag full of 15 pieces of charred spacecraft. He flew from Perth to Melbourne, then to Sydney, to Hawaii, and on to San Francisco. He was met at the airport by 40 reporters, and was whisked to the *Examiner*'s offices by limousine, beating the deadline by eight hours. The newspaper, to prove the debris was genuine, sent it to the NASA laboratories at Huntsville, Alabama, to be authenticated. After a week of testing, they said it couldn't be pieces of Skylab, as it was organic. At one stage, it was suggested that it might be spaceman poo. In the end, they took another look, and concluded it was balsa wood from the insulation.

With good grace, the newspaper paid up. Stan Thornton, who didn't have a clue as to what was going on around him, and the media scrum he was creating, was presented with the keys to the city of San Francisco, by mayor Dianne Feinstein, pocketed the cheque, and headed home. Balladonia's moment in the world spotlight burnt bright but, as always, eventually faded. But the incident continued to cause ripples, with conspiracy theories flying about. (Flying about, spacecraft ...did you see what I did there?)

John Summerville-Smith, a journalist for the *Toorak Times* had travelled to Kalgoorlie a few days before Skylab's re-entry. The Melbourne gossip columnist claimed he had been tipped off by the Americans as to where the crash site would be. He said the Yanks had told him a week before that the crash site would be in Laverton, about 240 miles from Kalgoorlie. Would you travel 3,000 kilometres by chance? Some reports suggest that the Skylab had deliberately been brought down over land so that secret military espionage equipment could be recovered. Now, Balladonia to Kalgoorlie is a 400-kilometre distance, which, in terms of the Australian outback, is just around the corner. Coincidence? No one knows the truth, but it's a good story nonetheless.

In 1992, 13 years after the crash, Pauline & Geoff Grewar were flying a small aircraft over their farm to inspect the property.

Some of these farms are the size of Belgium, don't forget. They spotted a metallic silver object, which at first they thought was a car that had been dumped on their property. On further inspection, it turned out to be the largest piece of Skylab ever recovered: an oxygen tank, that had laid there all that time.

The Australian outback is a large place. As of 2020, in it's metropolitan statistical area, New York has 24 million people living in it's confines. Australia, has 26 million people living in the whole country. There is a bit of space. The $400 littering fine was paid on the 30th anniversary of the crash by a US radio station. The cheque hangs in the Esperance Museum. There is still stuff out there. God's protection, and speed, treasure hunters.

Gold ceiling tiles.

And this is what I think happened back at Wedge tail roadhouse on the morning of the 12th of July 1979, the day after the re-entry disintegration of Skylab:

"Bruce, we've just had 80 metres of gold re-entry shield fall into the back paddock. What should I do with it?"

"Do you think we could make ceiling tiles out of it?"

"Sure, why not? Should keep the heat out."

"Noelene, fetch me a hammer."

They don't know what they have. They could be millionaires!

Chapter 12 – Epiphany

On the road again. From Balladonia to Norseman is only a couple of hours, Norseman being the point at which the Eyre Highway ends. By now, I thought news of my epic quest would have filtered through to the township, and I was quite expecting some school children to be lining the roadside, waving union jacks. Maybe some bunting overhead, a small brass band playing a medley of Beatles hits. But no. Nothing. You could turn right to go to Kalgoorlie or left to Esperance. There is not even a sign saying you've crossed the Nullarbor. Nothing. A bit of a let-down, if I'm honest. I turned left.

The town of Norseman takes its name from a horse called Hardy Norseman, owned by one Laurie Sinclair. One night in 1892, the horse was tethered to a tree. Overnight, it scraped away at the earth with a hoof to expose a gold nugget. That find led not only to more gold being found, but also to the discovery of one of the richest quartz reefs ever found in Australia. [used in the manufacture of glass, no, I didn't know either.]

As I entered Norseman, I quickly found Wilson's Diesel & Auto Repairs, which had been recommended to me the night before at Cocklebiddy as a place I might get the tyre fixed. The workshop was huge, with all sorts of tools and gadgets strewn all over the place. As my eyes adjusted to the gloom, I detected some movement in the far left corner. It turned out to be a chap called Graham, and he turned out to be a godsend. He was a small nugget of a man; the sort of car mechanic that you thought could climb inside the engine and fix the problems from there. I explained the flat tyre, and he stopped whatever he was doing, and started on my problem straight away.

As he was working away, other people would wander into the workshop and question him about all things mechanical, and he would answer with patience and good nature. At one point, a truck driver turned up at the front doors and shouted across, "Graham, I can't crack me nuts!" Sounded painful …

He knew all the answers to all the questions and appeared to have the appropriate tools to hand. The man was a genius. Ten minutes later he had fixed the tyre, and I asked him what the problem had been.

"Kangaroo bone," he said, with a straight face. He could sense that I thought he was taking the mickey, so he returned to his workbench, had a rummage, and produced a 10 mm shard of bone that was as hard as … well, bone, actually. "Get it all the time," said Graham. I was astonished that this tiny piece of bone had taken Wombat out. Mind you, there must be enough kangaroo skeletons on the highway to fill Fiji.

***

Back in the now fixed Wombat, I was heading 200 kilometres south to the town of Esperance, my hotel stop for the night.

Around the town of Salmon Gums, I suddenly noticed that the countryside had changed. There were fields of wheat, and hedgerows and flowers along the roadside. It was like I was driving through Suffolk or Norfolk in England. I half expected to see my father-in-law, a farmer, sitting on the back of a combine harvester, moaning about the weather. Always complaining, bloody farmers. Still, the new vistas made a pleasant change.

So, into Esperance I trundled, and I easily found the Comfort Inn suites. Very nice hotel; I could even order freshly-shucked oysters from room service. Quite a contrast from the schnitzel and steak knife the night before.

I took a stroll to the Visitor Centre, and the flies, realising I was fresh meat, went into a frenzy. If you were born in the town and grew up there, maybe you would get used to them. But slap my face and call me Judy, they were bloody annoying. As always, the staff in the Visitor Centre were friendly and knowledgeable. I had my questions answered, and strolled back along the seafront to my hotel. I passed a nice town beach, an imposing line of Norfolk Island pines, and children playing in a water park; all very pleasant. It gave the area a safe, happy feel. You could imagine that the people that live here would consider Bali as a viable holiday option, and could probably have a fair stab at making fresh pasta.

For my dining option that evening, I jumped into the car and drove a little way out of town to the Lucky Bay Brewing company – a hipster craft beer joint. It was all ankle boots and trilbies there, but they did have wood fired pizza, so I was happy. Very nice place.

Back at my hotel later that evening, I had an epiphany ... I had had enough of hotels and driving.

There was no real reason to continue on to Perth; I had been there before. I was missing my wife, and I had done what I set out to do:

drive across the Nullarbor. So, I was going to go home. With the decision made, I slept the sleep of the dead.

The next morning it was a lovely, bright, breezy day. With Wombat's liquids checked, I was going to visit a national park, then meander up to Norseman, stay the night, then attempt to do the whole of the Eyre Highway in a day. Nice to have things planned.

I drove east along the coast to the Cape Le Grand National Park. $15 to get in, ok I guess, but there was a lovely lady in the gatehouse, with suggestions on where to go and what to look for. Emus and kangaroos were easy to spot, and some of the vistas were outstanding, Lucky Bay being my favourite. After an hour or so, and with a couple of good photos in the bag, I headed back to Esperance and turned right to go up to Norseman. All morning I had been calling hotels there to get some accommodation, but no one would pick up. And they weren't cheap, either! I would call in when I arrived.

By the time I got there I was a tad peckish. A sandwich or roll would do. I found the main drag of the town. It was a really wide street, but everything appeared to be shut down. Even the doll museum had chains on its doors – a major disappointment. The large pub on the corner may or may not have been open. This place had a strange vibe. The sort of place that the producers of Michael Jackson's 'Thriller' music video may have considered as a dance routine space for zombies. There was one supermarket, which appeared to be open. Large metal doors with grills over the windows gave the impression of a prison, and there were large signs all over the door:

"School children not allowed between these hours."

"School children to leave bags outside."

"All school children are little thieving gits."

I think that's what they said. I entered the emporium and had to wait for a few seconds to let my eyes adjust to the gloom. The store was enormous, and it appeared to sell every product humanity had ever made. I found some hot dog buns that looked to be in date; now for some cheese. I asked a lady filling up the flip-flops stand. "Cheese? Should be over there by the ball bearings," she said.

Cheese found, my thoughts turned to coleslaw. I knew I was pushing the culinary boundaries of Norseman, but what the hell. By this time I was quite close to the front counter, so I asked the young lady working there where the coleslaw was. She physically took a step back, and she had a look on her face like I was going to attack her with a rusty hacksaw blade. But then I got a hint that she might be Spanish. If I had said to her, "Donde esta la ensalada de col?" she might have been able to help. (Look at me go!)

I returned to the flip-flop lady, who considered my question and said that, if they had any, it would be over in the corner, near the tractor seats. I made my purchases, the girl at the checkout keeping a very sharp eye on me.

Having snarfed the rolls, I considered my options. I was glad that I had not booked any accommodation here; I don't think I would be dining at a craft brewery in Norseman. So, I decided to make a run for Cocklebiddy, as it's only 400 kilometres. I re-joined the Eyre Highway and pointed Wombat east. I was heading home.

What I hadn't taken into consideration was that I was now going the opposite way on the time zones. So, when I got to the Wedge tail Inn, it was 7 pm and pitch black. Florence was on duty. "Kitchen closed. Kitchen closed," was her opening gambit, throwing her hands in the air as she spoke.

Luckily, I wasn't hungry. "Just a room for the night, please."

"Full up. Full up," she said.

She was just being a bag. I knew she had rooms, but I was knackered and in no mood to argue. "Can I just park round the back of the hotel, then, and sleep in the car?"

"$25, please," said Florence.

"No, you don't understand. I don't want a powered site, just a patch of grass to park off the highway."

"Still $25, and we will check." Charming people.

Anyway, I paid the money, drove around the back, joined the 30 or so other vehicles already in place, and settled down for the night. Around 2 am a wind started up, coming from the direction of the coast about 25 kilometres away. The temperature dropped very quickly. It was bloody freezing! The wind felt like it was coming from Antarctica. It probably was.

Chapter 13 – Heading east

I was awake early, and made my preparations to leave. As I visited the shower block, I noticed a huge aviary which, on closer inspection, revealed it contained two wedge-tailed eagles, both of whom had been injured in car crashes. Samantha and Bruce were their names, and up close and personal these creatures are magnificent. Much bigger than you think, from what you observe, as you pass them on the highway. It felt like if you were going to speak in their presence, you would have to whisper. I hope they were considered for the Australian national emblem. With their injuries they could not be released back into the wild, but they were obviously well looked after. I do hope that one day, if Florence was feeding them, she might fall over and render herself unconscious, and the raptors could peck her eyes out. I know she had rooms. Bag.

Steady as she goes, I pulled back onto the highway and headed east. There was a place

I wanted to call into near the border with South Australia, a place called Eucla. In researching the drive before I set off from Brisbane, I had stumbled onto this story, and I think it's a cracker.

Chapter 14 – The Nullarbor Nymph

Let's go back to Boxing Day 1971, and we are in the bar of the Eucla Motel, middle of bloody nowhere, Western Australia/South Australia border. Geoff Pearce, from Perth, is in the bar, heading towards Sydney to look for work. He can't pay his bill, but promises, through his contacts in the media, to put Eucla on the map. In the bar that day are a couple of professional kangaroo shooters, a fisherman, a bus driver, and the girlfriend of one of the marsupial killers. Over a lot of beer, they come up with a story of a long-haired, half naked woman living with the kangaroos in the bush. Deciding they needed some evidence, the pranksters shot a film on an old 8 mm camera.

Roo shooter Laurie Scott's girlfriend, Genice Brooker, agreed to dress up in freshly-killed kangaroo skins and run around the bush while the shaky amateur footage was shot. Don't forget, dear reader, this was in the age before the internet, but they sent the footage in to some TV stations and it went global. At this time, Eucla had a population of "eight people, four cross-bred dogs, and a swearing parrot."

Film crews from the BBC in London were dispatched, along with crews from the USA and Japan. The place was swamped with reporters.

Some of the locals got in on the act, trucking tourists and media personnel out into the bush to show them footprints of the Nymph, as she was now called. At one point, the owner of the motel considered building a tourist complex with a casino. Bush coach driver Bob Marshall convinced a bus-load of visitors that he had spotted a girl wearing a furry cloak, the passengers were so concerned for her wellbeing they left sandwiches and milk by the roadside.

One journalist, however, named Murray Nicholl, thought he smelled a hoax, and after a crazy 5 months, took Laurie out one evening for a drink and got him smashed.

"Of course it's all bullshit, mate," was his statement later.

The next day, the front page of the newspapers read "Nullarbor Nymph a hoax". Their time in the spotlight was over. But wow! One girl, running around the bush in animal skins, had kept the world's problems off the front page, not for a day, but for weeks. Absolutely brilliant, and all because of some good old boys sitting around drinking beer.

Chapter 15 – Nullarbor

Leaving Eucla, I made my way through the WA/SA border, and then had the bonus of driving along the top of the Bunda Cliffs, so on my right-hand side was the sea. At this point on the Eyre Highway you are closest to the Trans-Australian Railway. It's about 100 kilometres north of the road. Originally, back in 1917, you could only go from Kalgoorlie, WA, to Port Augusta, SA. When that section was completed, there were about 50 settlements along the track for maintenance workers and their families. A pretty isolated life. Imagine living in a shed, with no electricity, no air con, and living through an Australian summer. Bonkers!

When steam turned to diesel, the need for these workers died out. Today, the Indian Pacific is the only train to journey the full width of the continent. Named after the two seas it connects, you can go from Perth to Sydney, a 4,352-kilometre trip. Mind you, with tickets starting at $2,000 and going all the way up to $10,000, you would have to really like train journeys. It takes about four days, and has the longest straight piece of track in the world, a stretch of 478 kilometres.

(For the price they charge for the tickets, I would expect gold ceiling tiles.)

From the WA border to the Nullarbor Roadhouse is about 200 kilometres, and I called in for some photo opportunities. Every tourist normally stops here. Before the completion of the highway, the Nullarbor station covered 1.25 million acres (that's 2.7 times larger than Singapore), and had sheep, horses, and cattle roaming around. When then highway was installed, they started selling petrol to generate some extra income. With the addition of food and drinks over the years, the roadhouse has become a popular stopover.

The Nullarbor Plain, so named by surveyor EA Delisser in 1860, is Latin for 'no trees'. I always thought it was desert, but it is the world's largest, flattest piece of limestone in the world. Once part of the ocean floor, it covers an area of 200,000 square kilometres. You can see it from space. It's the same size as Nebraska and, for comparison's sake, the UK is 240,000 square kilometres. It's a big place.

After leaving the roadhouse, I was going to make a run to Port Augusta, in total doing about 1,200 kilometres for the day, from Cocklebiddy to Port Augusta, my longest drive on the trip. I had no desire to stop in Ceduna on the way back, the smell of nappies still fresh in my mind. It was a long day, my lower back was aching after sitting all day, and I arrived at my motel a little after 8 pm. 14 hours in the saddle. I didn't need much rocking that night.

So, dear reader, before we leave the Nullarbor Plain, there is something else to report. We have established that the plain is the biggest slab of limestone on the planet, but underneath, it is riddled with sinkholes and cave systems, some of the largest cave systems in the world. It's like a great big honeycomb. Some parts are filled with water. Salt water, unfortunately; otherwise, it could have come in handy for irrigation or watering stock. How these caves got there in the first place has had the geological bods stroking their beards for many years. Some think the caves were formed 30 million years ago, when Australia broke off of Antarctica and started drifting north.

Usual wisdom on caves is that they are formed by the erosion from running water, but as this area has never had a wet climate that's a non-starter. Another theory is that fresh water seeps down and reacts with the salt water but, as the Nullarbor only gets about six inches of rain a year and the underground lakes are about 90 to 100 metres down, that's a bit of a stretch also. In truth, no one knows for sure. One thing we do know is that, because the tectonic plates of the earth are very dormant in the area, the slab of limestone is still intact. If the

Nullarbor was in northern Australia, it would have been munched up and spat out by the moving surface of the earth, and would probably be a mountain range in Papua New Guinea by now.

Lets talk about Megafauna, I know you want to.

Megafauna is a term used by science to describe animals that roamed Australia during the Pleistocene epoch of earth's history. That period ran from 2.5 million years ago, to about 15,000 years ago – the world's last ice age. As the name suggests, the animals were big. Skeletons of these animals have been found over quite a large part of the continent; not so much in the north, where acidic soil rots the bones, but the compromise there is that there are rock paintings that depicts some of the fauna.

Some of the dry caves on the Nullarbor had remained untouched for tens of thousands of years and had the perfect climate to preserve bones. In 2002, eight complete skeletons of Thylacoleo Carnifex, a marsupial lion, were found on the Nullarbor. It was the largest carnivorous mammal ever to have existed in Australia, and about the size of a modern-day African lioness. The first discovery of the lion was in 1859, when bones were found at Lake Colongulac in Victoria. (Nice name for a lake …) Pound for pound, it is thought the marsupial lion probably had the strongest bite of any mammal that has ever existed.

At the same time as the lion existed, there were other massive beasts:

Diprotodon – a wombat the size of a rhinoceros. (Imagine hitting one of those late at night, driving through the fog on the way to Dubbo, to pick up some KFC, in a Toyota Camry),

Stirton's Thunder Bird – a 10-foot-high, emu-like bird,

Megalania – a 20-foot-long giant goanna (big lizard),

and, my absolute favourite,

Dromornis Planei, or 'the demon duck of doom'– another very large flightless bird.

It is generally regarded by the scientific community that these species died out 46,000 years ago. With modern technology now suggesting the Aboriginal people migrated to Australia around 65,000 years ago, man and megafauna would have crossed paths for about 20,000 years. Just thinking out loud here – how did all the big stuff die out, and then come back as smaller versions later? Bonkers. Another thing, you could pour three slabs of VB down my throat, and I still wouldn't go up against a 'demon duck of doom' with only a Boomerang for protection. Just saying.

Let's get our feet wet.

In the late 60s and early 70s, with the rising popularity of scuba diving and the increasing awareness of the vast underground water systems under the plains, someone came up with the brainwave of diving in the caves. Now, I have been a certified PADI Open Water Diver for 35 years, and I know the day you take the sport for granted is the day you get into trouble. Once, while diving in Turkey, my oxygen tank came away from my buoyancy jacket and fell off. That was fun. Things can go wrong very fast.

Also, back in the day, my wife and I were with a bunch of friends on an 'unusual activities' weekend, and whilst "adventure caving" at the Cheddar Gorge caves in Somerset, UK, I got stuck in a pothole. (I know, I know. "Not surprised, you fat bastard." I can read your minds.) To try and visualise what this would have been like underwater, with all the diving gear on, is the stuff of nightmares. I think to go cave diving you have to be a scone short of a high tea. Do one thing or the other. It would be like climbing Everest, getting to the top, and then doing a cooking demonstration. You just wouldn't do it, would you? Do one thing or the other.

Divers started to descend on the cave systems in increasing numbers. In 1973 and 1974, eight divers died. So, laws were passed, and now only certified, highly trained divers can experience the caves. The water in the caves has been certified as the clearest water on the planet, with divers saying the experience is like floating in outer space. The story of one such diving expedition follows.

Let's go back to November 1988. Petrol was $1 a litre, Kylie Minogue was 20 years old. Andrew Wight, a very experienced cave diver and explorer, led a team of 15 men and women to the Pannikin Cave system, not too far from our old friend Cocklebiddy. They had done some reconnaissance dives in previous years and, after months of planning, were going to try and dive up to 6 kilometres along the underwater passageways. They had 5 tonnes of equipment in total, what with camping gear and diving paraphernalia, and had to lower 1 tonne of apparatus down 50 metres through a hole in the limestone floor of the Nullarbor and into a cave area where they made base camp. From there, they would enter the water and dive 1 kilometre to a place called Concord Landing, which is four stories high and the length of several football pitches.

Most of the cave is dry, but has access to the flooded cave tunnels This huge cavern is directly underneath the highway. The three 'push divers' waited 24 hours to allow their bodies to adjust to the atmosphere, then continued for another 3 kilometres, only to find any further progress forward was blocked by fallen rock. So, they turned round and came back. I'm not sure what they hoped to find – a boulder of gold? A small aquatic colony of Oompa Loompas? – it does seem a bit of a faff, for not much reward. I suppose, though, they had been where no other human has been before. So, ok, I guess. To finish this story, I have to go off on a bit of a tangent, so bear with.

In Aboriginal mythology, there is a story about the Rainbow Serpent. All of the different Aboriginal clans, all over the continent, have a version. The serpent created the world, and life, and when a rainbow occurs, it is the snake leaving one watering hole for another. It is the oldest deity worshipped on the planet. If you upset the serpent, though, it can cause absolute chaos. The Rainbow Serpent has been depicted in cave paintings all over Australia.

Back to our divers. When they first arrived, and started moving equipment into the cave mouth, they spotted a large snake. When they came to leave, they realised the snake had followed them down into the cave at base camp. When people passed by, it would rear up, but not strike.

At the campground up top, as they were preparing to help lift all the gear back up, they realised they were going to be hit by a once in 10- or 20-year weather phenomenon: a mini cyclone. There were winds of up to 150 kilometres an hour, and two years' worth of rain fell in 25 minutes. At the cave entrance, which was just a hole on the Nullarbor's surface, it was likened to bathwater going down a plughole. The weight of all the water made the cave entrance collapse, and the 13 people still inside had to run for their lives from the avalanche of thousands of tonnes of rock. It took 27 hours to get everyone out safely, and miraculously no one was injured. Had they disturbed the serpent? Should they be there? Were they in sacred places? Seems like a bit of a coincidence to me – a cyclone, just as you are leaving? There are places in Australia that are very mysterious, and should not be messed with, that's my conclusion. Maybe no one knew that these places are sacred, but I suppose they could have asked the Aboriginal peoples of the area first.

In the USA, would you go hiking through a Native American burial ground? No, you wouldn't. It would certainly make me think twice about just visiting the caves, let alone diving through them.

The story of the cave rescue was reported, and the movies come calling.

James Cameron, the Canadian film maker responsible for *Titanic* and *Avatar*, got to hear about the Pannikin Cave story and produced a film called *Sanctum*, which was released in 2010, loosely based on the events on the Nullarbor. It grossed $100 million at the box office. Not bad. Andrew Wight, the expedition leader, not only became a friend of Cameron's, but served as technical adviser on both films and real-life adventures. Andrew Wight produced over 45 films, all of which were concerned with underwater stories. He was awarded the Australian Geographic Society 'Spirit of Adventure' award in 1989. Ironically, after all of the diving he had done all over the world, he unfortunately died whilst piloting a helicopter in 2012, on his way to film the launch of a submarine. Also on board was American underwater cameraman Mike deGruy, another leading light in the underwater film family. Cameron had just appointed Wight as head of his 3D production operation in Sydney when the crash occurred. In 2012, Cameron dived to the deepest part of the ocean floor on earth, the Mariana Trench. He dived nearly 11 kilometres, and it took him 2 hours and 36 minutes to get down. He spent three hours on the seabed, then it took an hour and 10 minutes to get back up. If mount Everest were placed in the trench, there would still be 2,000 metres of water above it. So, he mucked about a bit, took a few samples of the seabed, stuff like that, and then came back up. Again, bit of a faff and not much reward for the millions of dollars spent, but an incredible adventure none the less. One slightly upsetting aspect of this tale though, is that, at the bottom of the Mariana trench, one of the most remotest areas of our planet, they found litter on the seabed. Humanity. Jesus. Well, I've been underwater and underground for far too long. Let's get driving again.

Chapter 16 – Port Augusta to Broken Hill

The next day was going to be an easy day, just a four-and-a-half-hour drive back to Broken Hill. So, I took it easy with my departure routine, enjoying the lovely, bright, breezy morning. I did wonder if the breeze was coming from the wind turbines, which I passed as I left Port Augusta and headed back through the Flinders Ranges. I decided right then and there that this section of the trip, Port Augusta to Broken Hill, was my favourite part of the trip.

At some point as I left the Ranges there was a bit of a commotion on the road up ahead. I noticed about 30 or 40 crows all chowing down on a fresh roo smorgasbord. The kangaroo looked as if it had swallowed Semtex and then been detonated. The poor marsupial had been transformed into small chunks and spread over about 75 metres. No wonder the crows were causing a fuss. They wouldn't have to look for food for the rest of the day, they could just waddle about and squawk ... a bit like Arsenal supporters.

Having time on my side, I could call into some attractions along the way. I stopped at the Giant Gum Tree of Orroroo – not especially tall, but enormous around the trunk.[A bit like me, some would say.] Said to be over 500 years old, it's older than the USA. I was a little disappointed there wasn't a souvenir stand selling 'I've seen big gums' T-shirts, or 'Look at my girth' tea towels, but hey, you can't have everything.

Coffee was calling, so I stopped in Peterborough, glad it was a bit warmer than the previous week. Originally called Petersburg, after Peter Doecke sold land to create the town in 1875. It was one of 69 towns in South Australia that were renamed, due to anti-German sentiment, during WWI. Jeez, they must have really disliked the Germans. Fair enough if you lived in, say, Kaiser Wilhelm-Ville, west Franz Ferdinand, or Red Baron Heights, by all means, change the name. But Petersburg? Come on. And it's in Russia.

I asked a chap on the main street for directions to an establishment selling coffee. Without doubt, the gentleman I spoke to had one of the strangest displays of facial hair I have ever seen. It's a little difficult to describe. Imagine if you will, dear reader, an old-school ruler.

Now imagine gluing that to the tip of your chin, so that it dangled towards your stomach. Now click your fingers, and it changes to white hair. And now lacquer it with hairspray so it doesn't move in the breeze, and voila! It was a one foot by one inch, completely straight, rectangle. If he had gone for a part in *The Lord of the Rings*, he wouldn't have had to have read for the part. Anyway, he directed me to 'The 229 on Main', and I'm so glad he did. It used to be a theatre, but is now a cafe, with all sorts of memorabilia and antiques. There were posters, vintage cameras, an old taxi, a statue of Marilyn Monroe, a WWII Jeep, and life-size figurines of the Blues Brothers, and why not? The sort of place *American Pickers* could do a whole show from. The coffee wasn't bad either. What a great place. Please stop in if you are passing; places like this need to be supported.

***

Back in the saddle, and another couple of hours later I was almost in Broken Hill. I had no hesitation in booking the Argent Motel again. As you approach the town from the west, there is a sign welcoming you, and hoping you have a good visit. And then, in brackets, it says, "It's on the left". Excellent. As if, after driving for hours across featureless plains, you would miss a settlement of 17,000 people.

I passed the enormous cemetery again, and made a stop at the visitor information centre for various enquiries. The chap who dealt with my questions knew everything about the town. He said that some university bods had done a survey of the cemetery in 2012 and estimated that there were approximately 50,000 people buried there. Try and picture that, 50,000 graves, now try and Imagine that in your village churchyard in the UK.

I had one question left for the visitor information centre guy, and I thought it might stump him. "Is there a collective noun for wedge-tailed eagles?" I had him, he didn't know. "It's a convocation", I said. (I did look it up before I asked, so I could act like a bit of smartarse. Something I've been doing for many years, according to my wife.)

Anyway, while we are on the subject, it's:

a wisdom of wombats

a parade of echidnas

a mob of kangaroos

a murder of crows

and a paddle of platypuses.

Lovely.

(I wonder what a group of nomad Harley-Davidson riders would be called … a 'knob' perhaps)

It was a gorgeous afternoon so, after checking into the hotel, I took a small drive 25 kilometres north to Silverton. No visit to Broken Hill is complete without this detour. As the name suggests, it was once a silver mine, opened in 1882, and operated for almost 100 years. At its peak, it employed close to 200 people, some as young as eight. Now, in the small settlement, there is an iconic pub, The Silverton Hotel, which is the main hub for tourists. Inside, you can see photos from some of the movies that were made in the area.

These include:

A Town Like Alice

Razorback

Mission: Impossible II

Mad Max 2

and *The Adventures of Priscilla, Queen of the Desert.*

Across from the pub there is a small Mad Max museum, trying to get the last dollar it possibly can out of the movie. There are a couple of art studios, you can ride a camel; that sort of thing. All in all, a pleasant area to visit. I drove on a few more kilometres to the Mundi Mundi Lookout. The view from here is truly spectacular; biblical, even. They say you can see the curvature of the earth. I couldn't, but pretended I could.

The sort of place you might bump into Charlton Heston wearing an old bed sheet and carrying some stone tablets, or even U2 doing a music video; it's that good.

***

Back at the hotel, I noticed a few rooms had been taken over by grey nomad bikers. Their very shiny, and very large motorbikes, were all proudly standing in a row. Now, I'm sure that the drivers are all nice people, but they do give the impression that they think they are a little bit special.

If you have ever witnessed some male nomad bikers prepare for a ride, it goes something like this:

First of all, push the electric starter motor on your $40,000 Harley Fat Boy.

Stand back and admire. (Don't forget, you've worked 27 years as a forklift driver in a paint distribution centre to save up for this.)

Lean over a share a small joke with your mate 'Spud'.

Admire for five to seven minutes. Make sure everybody within a 15-kilometre radius is either awake or pissed off by that throbbing engine sound. Periodically, lean over and give it some throttle.

Make sure you are wearing a white T-shirt, with some obscure rock band's insignia on it. (This has to be heavy metal. It can't be, say, Barbra Streisand or Barry Manilow.) Slip into a black leather bomber jacket. Tilt your head back slightly, so you can place the black crash helmet over your shoulder-length grey hair. (There will be some obscure travel sticker on the back of the helmet, like "I've seen the Yaks of Ulaanbaatar", or "I've dropped a cog at the great wall". This all adds to the mystique.) Lean over and give it a little throttle. Slip on your $7 Kmart imitation Ray Ban Wayfarers. Stand back and admire. Give it a little throttle. Slide one leg over the seat, and nonchalantly flick the kick stand back into place. Give a little throttle. Gently walk backwards on the bike until you have enough room to propel forward. Give a little throttle.

Make sure everyone in the vicinity can witness such majesty as yourself, controlling so much power. As you pull off down the road, leave your left leg dangling and, ever so slowly, over a period of, say, 10 seconds, lift it into position. Everything is good with the world; you are Johnny Big Potatoes. Knobs.

***

After my evening meal down on the main drag, I was strolling back up to my motel, enjoying the peace and quiet of the deserted town when, suddenly, what looked like a coach party of pensioners, all dragging wheelie luggage, started pouring into the high street from a side road. As I was the only person around, the first group of little grey-haired people made a beeline for me.

"Do you know where the Desert Sand Motor Inn is?" a little old lady asked, somewhat desperately. Now, as this was my second time in Broken Hill, and with a little help from Google Maps, I was able to help. "Down there, second on your left." Quite a crowd gathered around me. "No pushing, please. You will all get a turn", I said. I dispatched people left, right, and centre. The last group of three asked the question that I hoped I would get asked, as I had just done some research on it. "Could you tell us please, where is Mario's Palace Hotel?"

I let them have it with both barrels, 'say hello to my little friend' style. "You mean the place that Alfred Dunn designed in 1889 for the temperance movement; the place featured in *Priscilla;* the place with all the murals over the walls and the ceilings, the first one painted by owner Mario Celotto? Just down there on the left hand side."

As I turned and strutted off, I left them a little open-mouthed.

"Bet he has a Harley Fat Boy," I could see them thinking.

Chapter 17 – One of the food capitals of the world ... Gilgandra

I was going a slightly different way home. I had noticed that I could do a little detour and miss out Dubbo completely. Five hours after leaving Broken Hill, I stopped for lunch in the town of Cobar. As with so many towns in rural and remote Australia, Cobar had been founded on mining. This time, it was copper. Today, around 4,000 people call it home. And how about this, my Aussie amigos: established in 2003, the local council supports a local currency called the 'Cobar Quid'. It is produced by the Royal Australian Mint, and tries to encourage people to shop locally. So, a town you've never heard of, that you don't know where it is, with its own currency. Brilliant.

Leaving Cobar and its quids behind, I next called into the town of Nyngan, as I noticed it had a visitor information centre, and I wanted to check my directions. In 1990, I learned from displays on the walls of the centre, the whole town flooded, and all of the residents had to be helicoptered out. The local river had risen 5 metres, and 2,300 townsfolk had to be airlifted to safety. It is the biggest rescue mission ever carried out in New South Wales, and at one stage they thought about contacting Thunderbirds, it was that bad. There is an Iroquois helicopter, donated to the town by the federal government to commemorate the evacuation, which sits proudly outside the visitor centre. (The same sort of helicopters, I think, that were used in the opening scenes of *MASH*.)

I asked my questions to a couple of lovely ladies in the centre, and as I was leaving, they asked me where I was from. In my very best Dick Van Dyke fake cockney accent, I replied, "Good old London town, my lady. God bless you, Mary Poppins." I left to the sound of much laughter; don't think they get many people impersonating Disney chimney sweeps from 1910 in Nyngan.

I was heading to the village of Nevertire, where I would turn left to miss out Dubbo, and head for Gilgandra. In Nevertire I stopped at a pub to check directions. The pub had obviously just been recently renovated. It was very modern, a very 'white wine spritzer' sort of a place. It was empty apart from two female members of staff.

I ordered a Coke from the girl behind the bar, who had the physique of an East German Olympic javelin thrower. When she turned around to get my purchase from the fridge, I noticed she had a four-inch steel tube pieced through the skin at the back of her neck. As I was standing there, somewhat open-mouthed, the other girl, who was tapping away at a computer at the bar, asked me where I was from. "Just east of London," says I. "So am I. I'm from Romford," she replied. This being a town about 25 kilometres away from my hometown of Chelmsford, what were the chances? Well, we sang some Chaz and Dave songs, had some John Bull Bitter, and some jellied eels, and had a right old knees-up. Actually, none of that happened. But it could have. My second London incident of the day. Wow.

On I travelled to Gilgandra, my stop for the night. I found my hotel, the Silver Oaks, and it was very good; spotlessly clean. As this was potentially the last night of my trip, I thought I would celebrate with a nice meal. I consulted Google. Not a lot. I went back to reception and asked the mid-twenties Indian guy, who appeared to be in charge of the hotel, for any dining recommendations. "Royal Hotel," he said, and he gave me a knowledgeable nod, as if he were imparting some insider information that only special people receive.

I drove into the town centre and found the hotel. As I entered, I passed three grey nomad couples sitting quietly, with expectant looks on their faces. "Do you have a menu I could look at?" I said with a smile to the purple-haired, tattooed, nose-ring-wearing member of staff. "On the wall, and we don't open till six." She spoke to me like I was a full bedpan. The nomads were all waiting to place their orders, bless them.

There was nothing on the menu I wanted to eat, so plan B. There were two Chinese restaurants in town, apparently; that would do. The first one had shut down, and the second had obviously been a funeral company's head office at some point in its life, such was the architecture and the vibe. Plan C. Back on the main drag I found a café/bistro/diner sort of a place, but they did have a list of pizzas on a chalkboard.

I asked the harassed-looking lady, "I know it's not on your list, but could I just have a cheese pizza, please?" She seemed to be very confused by this request. "What, nothing but cheese?" It was probably the first time in her career that she hadn't put an order through to the kitchen that didn't involve meat. So unusual was my request that they didn't have a price for it on the till.

I suggested $16, and she accepted my proposal.

Back at my hotel, I opened the box. Hold the phone, Mabel. Jesus, how to describe it? Just a box of melted cheese; not sure if there was a base in there anywhere at all. The melted curd went up the interior of the box an inch on all sides. Must have been 2 kg of cheese in there to produce such a tsunami of fromage. By tilting the box, I could make a slow-motion mozzarella wave. I waited till it cooled down a bit, and solidified, I could then start slicing bits of cheese off. "I will dream well tonight," I thought.

I think it's pretty much taken as gospel these days that if you eat cheese before bedtime it can produce some pretty whacked-out, Willy Wonka-esque dreams. In England, when writer, producer, and billionaire Andrew Lloyd Webber cast Michael Crawford, the slapstick comedian from *Some Mothers Do 'Ave 'Em*, as the lead in *The Phantom of the Opera*, most put it down to eating blue cheese just before bed. There can be no other explanation.

Did I dream that night? Yes, vividly. I was whale watching, with Wombat beside me, and she said, "I don't want to be called Wombat anymore."

"What do you want to be called, then?" I asked.

She looked into the distance and, with a faraway look in her headlights, said, "Desert Warrior."

My car had a new name. Anyway, I don't think that Gilgandra will be featuring on any New South Wales foodie trails any time soon. Mind you, the Meat Lovers Pizza Appreciation Society should put it on their radar.

Chapter 18 – Last push home

The next morning, I was eager to get on the road and head home. Not that I had done anything special, I'd just taken a long drive, but it would be good to see my wife, have a coffee from my own mug, and sleep in my own bed. After checking the Wom … sorry, Desert Warrior's fluids, I set off north up the A39. I drove through miles of roadwork's (great to see them again), through Moree, through Boggabilla (I did wave at the walking shit flies as I passed, but got no response), and as I re-entered Queensland at Goondiwindi, I called into the town for a coffee.

OK, competition time.

What does Goondiwindi mean, in the local Bigambul Aboriginal language, yes, you've guessed it ,

Duck Poo.

Now, I get the trend for places to revert to their original names, like Ayers rock to Uluru, and Frazer Island to K'gari, that's all fine. But what a difference it would make to the town if it were called 'Duck Poo'. People would travel miles, maybe even internationally, to get a selfie with the town sign. Tourism would go through the roof. Imagine the souvenir tee shirt opportunities, 'I got drunk and slipped over in Duck Poo' or 'shit happens in Duck Poo', or to use Tasmania's latest promotional tourist sound bite, 'come down for the air, and smell the Duck Poo.' The possibilities are endless. You could 'twin' the town with other strange sounding towns around the globe, maybe, Goose pimple junction, Ohio, or Poo Poo point, Washington, or my favourite, Shit, Mazandaran province, Iran.

The area where Goondiwindi now stands, was first settled in the late 1840's, as a cattle station, but there was continual skirmishes with the local Aboriginal people. In 1849, after two cattlemen were killed, a group of 22 ,including 12 mounted 'native police' attacked a large group of Aboriginal warriors, at a place called Carbuckey, about 15 kms to the west. 100 indigenous people were killed, and, not surprisingly, broke the back of any further resistance.

Now, this is something I didn't know about Australian history. 'Native' police were Aboriginal men that were drafted into police force, with the hope that their presence would help keep the peace. The government funded corps, operated from 1837 to 1915, and in the course for their duties were responsible for hundreds of deaths of their own people. Obviously though, they were under the direction of white police captains. Quite a few countries around the world have some dark skeletons in their closets.

After England's Queen Victoria proclaimed Queensland a new colony in 1859, Goondiwindi became a bona fide border crossing from New South Wales. In 1880 they built a bridge across the Macintyre river, and installed a customs house, to gather taxes from goods moved interstate.

The customs house still stands, and is now a museum. The need to collect taxes ceased in 1901, with the federation of the 6 Australian states. Today around 6,500 people call Duck Poo home.

I drove out of Goondiwindi, on to and around Toowoomba, and arrived at my home in Brisbane at 4 pm. As I got out of the car I stood for a moment, looked at the warrior, and nodded my head, briefly, as a mark of respect.

Conclusions;

To drive across the Nullarbor is a bit of a breeze, really. It's not difficult at all. If you enjoy driving, it's a blast. It certainly wasn't what I was expecting. I loved it.

Imagine driving between London and Syria, or from Washington, DC, to Los Angeles, and there being nothing in between except a few petrol stations. Bloody fantastic! In total, I did a little over 8000kms, in nine and a half days.

Respect to the grey nomad community out there, it sounds like a romantic notion, driving all over Australia, to be out on the road, but it can be hard.

The sense of peace and childlike wonder I felt being out there will stay with me for a long time. I'm sure all the things I saw and experienced, and the stories I uncovered, would not have happened if I hadn't seen that travel programme on the BBC back in the day. Thank you, Simon Calder.

Would I do it again? At the drop of a hat.

P.S. If anybody is in the market for 750 ml of power steering fluid, please email me.

About the Author

Retiring to Australia, after 20 years working on the international money markets in both London and New York, the author remembers a travel programme from England and decides to hop in his 20 year old Toyota called wombat and drive across Australia.

References

Chapter 6 references History of Dubbo- Wikipedia

Chapter 7 Dubbo to Broken Hill- Wikipedia

Chapter 9 Eyre highway- Wikipedia, abc.anu.edu.au

Chapter 11 Skylab- Forbes.com, Wikipedia, SFgate.com, Nytimes.com, Watoday.com.au, abc.net.au

Chapter 14 Nullarbor Nymph- Wikipedia, Australiangeographiceuclastay.com.au, Nullarbarroadhouse.com.au,

Chapter 15 Nullarbor and diving- Australia.com, Wikipedia, westerrnaustralia.com, museumvictoria.com.au, nullarborroadhouse.com.au, Nullarbor dreaming video, adelaidenow.com.au, cavediving.com.au

Printed in Great Britain
by Amazon